To:

_____

From:

_____

Date:

_____

© 2010 Summerside Press™
Minneapolis 55438
www.summersidepress.com

When God thinks of you...He smiles

A *Pocket Inspirations* Book

ISBN 978-1-60936-020-7

All rights reserved. No part of this book may be reproduced in any form
without permission in writing from the publisher.

Scripture references are from the following sources: The Holy Bible,
King James Version (KJV). The Holy Bible, New International Version®,
NIV®. Copyright © 1973, 1978, 1984 by International Bible Society.
Used by permission of Zondervan. All rights reserved worldwide. The
New King James Version (NKJV). Copyright © 1982 by Thomas Nelson,
Inc. Used by permission. The New American Standard Bible® (NASB),
Copyright © 1960, 1962, 1963, 1968, 1971, 1972, 1973, 1975, 1977,
1995 by The Lockman Foundation. Used by permission. The New
Revised Standard Version Bible (NRSV). Copyright 1989, 1995, Division
of Christian Education of the National Council of the Churches of
Christ in the United States of America. Used by permission. The Holy
Bible, New Living Translation (NLT), copyright 1996, 2004. Used by
permission of Tyndale House Publishers, Inc., Wheaton, Illinois. *The
Message.* Copyright © 1993, 1994, 1995, 1996, 2000, 2001, 2002 by
Eugene Peterson. Used by permission of NavPress, Colorado Springs,
CO. *The Living Bible* (TLB) © 1971. Used by permission of Tyndale
House Publishers, Inc., Wheaton, Illinois 60189. The Amplified®
Bible (AMP), © 1954, 1958, 1962, 1964, 1965, 1987 by The Lockman
Foundation. Used by permission. All rights reserved.

Compiled by Connie Troyer
Cover and interior design by Mick Thurber Design

*Summerside Press™ is an inspirational publisher offering fresh,
irresistible books to uplift the heart and engage the mind.*

Printed in USA.

When God thinks of you...
He smiles

PROMISES FOR LIFE

summerside
PRESS™

You Are Significant!

So God created people in his own image;
God patterned them after himself.

GENESIS 1:27 NLT

As God's workmanship, we deserve
to be treated, and to treat ourselves,
with affection and affirmation,
regardless of our appearance or performance.

MARY ANN MAYO

Every one of us as human beings is
known and loved by the Creator apart
from every other human on earth.

JAMES DOBSON

God loves me as God loves all people—
without qualification.

ROBERTA BONDI

Stand outside this evening. Look at the stars.
Know that you are special and loved
by the One who created them.

All that we have and are is one of the unique and
never-to-be repeated ways God has chosen to
express Himself in space and time. Each of us,
made in His image and likeness, is yet another
promise He has made to the universe that
He will continue to love it and care for it.

BRENNAN MANNING

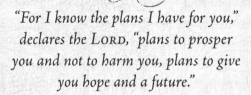

*"For I know the plans I have for you,"
declares the LORD, "plans to prosper
you and not to harm you, plans to give
you hope and a future."*

JEREMIAH 29:11 NIV

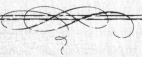

God Delights in You

You'll get a brand-new name straight from
the mouth of God. You'll be a stunning
crown in the palm of God's hand, a jeweled
gold cup held high in the hand of your God.
No more will anyone call you Rejected, and
your country will no more be called Ruined.
You'll be called Hephzibah (My Delight),
and your land Beulah (Married),
because God delights in you.

ISAIAH 62:2–4 MSG

God has mercies to give, and He intends to
give them to us; those mercies are not broken
pieces or someone else's leftovers.... God has
bags that were never untied, never opened up,
but set aside through a thousand generations
for those who hope in His mercy.

JOHN BUNYAN

By this I know that You favor and delight in
me, because my enemy does not triumph over
me. And as for me, You have upheld me in my
integrity and set me in Your presence forever.

PSALM 41:11–12 AMP

He [God] delights to meet the faith of one who
looks up to Him and says, "Lord, You know that
I cannot do this—but I believe that You can!"

AMY CARMICHAEL

For the LORD takes delight in his people;
he crowns the humble with salvation.

PSALM 149:4 NIV

Something to Count On

Do you believe that God is near? He wants
you to. He wants you to know that He is in
the midst of your world. Wherever you are
as you read these words, He is present.
In your car. On the plane. In your office,
your bedroom, your den, He's near.
And He is more than near. He is active.

MAX LUCADO

If you believe in God, it is not too difficult to
believe that He is concerned about the universe
and all the events on this earth. But the really
staggering message…is that this same God cares
deeply about you and your identity and the
events of your life.

All the world is an utterance of the Almighty.
Its countless beauties, its exquisite adaptations,
all speak to you of Him.

PHILLIPS BROOKS

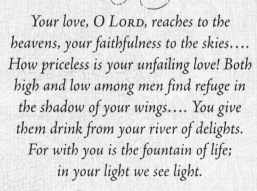

Your love, O LORD, reaches to the heavens, your faithfulness to the skies.... How priceless is your unfailing love! Both high and low among men find refuge in the shadow of your wings.... You give them drink from your river of delights. For with you is the fountain of life; in your light we see light.

PSALM 36:5, 7–9 NIV

His Unchanging Love

Nothing we can do will make God love us less;
nothing we do can make Him love us more. He
loves us unconditionally with an everlasting love.
All He asks of us is that we respond to Him with
the free will that He has given to us.

NANCIE CARMICHAEL

God's love is unchangeable. He loves us in spite of
knowing us as we really are. Were it not for the love
of God, none of us would ever have a chance.

BILLY GRAHAM

All the things in this world are gifts
and signs of God's love to us. The whole
world is a love letter from God.

PETER KREEFT

What gives me hope is knowing God's
character, knowing what He's like…and that
He doesn't change. Therefore, no matter
what changes in my life, no matter what
the circumstances are, I don't have to lose
hope, because I'm not trusting in my life, I'm
trusting in the One who holds my life: God.

LISA WHELCHEL

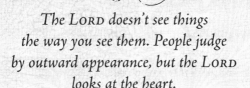

*The LORD doesn't see things
the way you see them. People judge
by outward appearance, but the LORD
looks at the heart.*

1 SAMUEL 16:7 NLT

God's Place for You

Where you are right now is God's place for you.
Live and obey and love and believe right there.

1 CORINTHIANS 7:17 MSG

Left to our own agendas, we either run at
breakneck speeds right past the pasture...
or sit in the parched desert. The Shepherd...
intervenes on our behalf to guide us...onto a
quiet path and into a calmer faith.

PATSY CLAIRMONT

What God does in time, He planned
from eternity. And all that He planned in
eternity He carries out in time.... No part
of His eternal plan changes.

J. I. PACKER

The steps of a man are established by the LORD,
and He delights in his way.

PSALM 37:23 NASB

Live for today but hold your hands open to
tomorrow. Anticipate the future and its changes
with joy. There is a seed of God's love in every
event, every circumstance, every unpleasant
situation in which you may find yourself.... Allow
your dreams a place in your prayers and plans.
God-given dreams can help you move into the
future He is preparing for you.

BARBARA JOHNSON

*The LORD will work out his plans
for my life—for your faithful love,
O LORD, endures forever.*

PSALM 138:8 NLT

A Work of Art

Each one of us is God's special work of art. Through us, He teaches and inspires, delights and encourages, informs and uplifts all those who view our lives. God, the master artist, is most concerned about expressing Himself—His thoughts and His intentions—through what He paints in our character.... [He] wants to paint a beautiful portrait of His Son in and through your life. A painting like no other in all of time.

JONI EARECKSON TADA

Every person ever created is so special that their presence in the world makes it richer and fuller and more wonderful than it could ever have been without them.

Whether we are poets or parents or teachers
or artists or gardeners, we must start where
we are and use what we have. In the process
of creation and relationship, what seems
mundane and trivial may show itself to be
holy, precious, part of a pattern.

LUCI SHAW

God gives everyone a special gift
and a special place to use it.

*How great are your works, O LORD,
how profound your thoughts!*

PSALM 92:5 NIV

His Wisdom and Love

I try to avoid looking forward or backward,
and try to keep looking upward.

CHARLOTTE BRONTË

Few delights can equal the mere presence
of one whom we trust utterly.

GEORGE MACDONALD

God loves you! It's not complicated or
conditional—it's just a fact! Our human
understanding can't comprehend the reason why,
only that it's true. As much as you might want
to explain it, dissect it, reason it out, you just can't.
Instead of wrapping yourself in questions,
wrap yourself in His love.

REBECCA CURRINGTON

His overflowing love delights to make us partakers
of the bounties He graciously imparts.

HANNAH MORE

This is the real gift: you have been given
the breath of life, designed with a unique,
one-of-a-kind soul that exists forever—
the way that you choose to live it doesn't
change the fact that you've been given
the gift of being now and forever.
Priceless in value, you are handcrafted
by God, who has a personal design
and plan for each of us.

WENDY MOORE

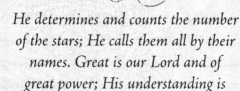

*He determines and counts the number
of the stars; He calls them all by their
names. Great is our Lord and of
great power; His understanding is
inexhaustible and boundless.*

PSALM 147:4-5 AMP

Child of God

You are a child of your heavenly Father.
Confide in Him. Your faith in His love
and power can never be bold enough.

BASILEA SCHLINK

When we call on God, He bends down
His ear to listen, as a father bends down
to listen to his little child.

ELIZABETH CHARLES

He only is the Maker
of all things near and far;
He paints the wayside flower,
He lights the evening star;
the wind and waves obey Him,
by Him the birds are fed;
much more to us, His children,
He gives our daily bread.

MATTHIAS CLAUDIUS

Remember you are very special to God as
His precious child. He has promised to
complete the good work He has begun in you.
As you continue to grow in Him, He will
make you a blessing to others.

You are in the Beloved...therefore infinitely dear
to the Father, unspeakably precious to Him.

NORMAN F. DOWTY

That Hand which bears all nature up
Shall guard His children well.

WILLIAM COWPER

*What marvelous love the Father has
extended to us! Just look at it—
we're called children of God!*

1 JOHN 3:1 MSG

God-Provision

At the very heart of the universe
is God's desire to give.

Steep yourself in God-reality, God-initiative,
God-provisions. You'll find all your everyday
human concerns will be met. Don't be afraid of
missing out. You're my dearest friends! The Father
wants to give you the very kingdom itself.

LUKE 12:31–32 MSG

Your Father knows that you need these things.
But seek His kingdom, and these things will be
added to you. Do not be afraid, little flock, for your
Father has chosen gladly to give you the kingdom.

LUKE 12:30–32 NASB

The well of Providence is deep.
It's the buckets we bring to it that are small.

MARY WEBB

All that is good, all that is true, all that is beautiful,
all that is beneficent, be it great or small,
be it perfect or fragmentary, natural as well as
supernatural, moral as well as material,
comes from God.

CARDINAL JOHN HENRY NEWMAN

All perfect gifts are from above
and all our blessings show
the amplitude of God's dear love,
which any heart may know.

LAURA LEE RANDALL

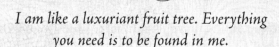

I am like a luxuriant fruit tree. Everything
you need is to be found in me.

HOSEA 14:8 MSG

Fresh Insights

With God, life is eternal—both in quality and
length. There is no joy comparable to the joy
of discovering something new from God,
about God. If the continuing life is a life of joy,
we will go on discovering, learning.

EUGENIA PRICE

This life is not all. It is an "unfinished symphony"...
with those who know that they are related to God
and have felt the power of an endless life.

HENRY WARD BEECHER

Every day we live is a priceless gift of God,
loaded with possibilities to learn something new,
to gain fresh insights.

DALE EVANS ROGERS

I love those who love me; and those who
diligently seek me will find me.

PROVERBS 8:17 NASB

God is not an elusive dream or a phantom to
chase, but a divine person to know. He does not
avoid us, but seeks us. When we seek Him, the
contact is instantaneous.

NEVA COYLE

*So let us know, let us press on to know the
LORD.... He will come to us like the rain,
like the spring rain watering the earth.*

HOSEA 6:3 NASB

God Is Enough

He who has God and everything has no more
than he who has God alone.

C. S. LEWIS

God, of Your goodness give me Yourself,
for You are enough for me. And only
in You do I have everything.

JULIAN OF NORWICH

Nothing can separate you from His love,
absolutely nothing.... God is enough for time,
and God is enough for eternity. God is enough!

HANNAH WHITALL SMITH

To know Him is to love Him and to know Him better is to love Him more. We can get a right start only by accepting God as He is and learning to love Him for what He is. As we go on to know Him better we shall find it a source of unspeakable joy that God is just what He is.... O God, I have tasted Thy goodness, and it has both satisfied me and made me thirsty for more.

A.W. Tozer

As the deer pants for streams of water,
so my soul pants for you, O God. My soul
thirsts for God, for the living God.

Psalm 42:1–2 niv

God Is Our Refuge

Whom have I in heaven but You? And besides
You, I desire nothing on earth. My flesh and
my heart may fail, but God is the strength
of my heart and my portion forever.... As for
me, the nearness of God is my good; I have
made the Lord GOD my refuge.

PSALM 73:25–26, 28 NASB

If the Lord be with us, we have no cause to fear.
His eye is upon us, His arm over us, His ear
open to our prayer.

ANDREW MURRAY

GOD's strong name is our help,
the same GOD who made heaven and earth.

PSALM 124:8 MSG

When God has become...our refuge
and our fortress, then we can reach out
to Him in the midst of a broken world
and feel at home while still on the way.

HENRI J. M. NOUWEN

The LORD is a shelter for the oppressed,
a refuge in times of trouble.
Those who know your name trust in you,
for you, O LORD, do not abandon those
who search for you.
Sing praises to the LORD
who reigns in Jerusalem.
Tell the world about his unforgettable deeds....
He does not ignore the cries of those
who suffer.

PSALM 9:9–12 NLT

Connected through Prayer

No matter where we are,
God can hear us from there!

And then a little laughing prayer
Came running up the sky,
Above the golden gutters, where
The sorry prayers go by.
It had no fear of anything,
But in that holy place
It found the very throne of God
And smiled up in His face.

Amy Carmichael

They who seek the throne of grace
Find that throne in every place;
If we live a life of prayer,
God is present everywhere.

Oliver Holden

To pray is to change. This is a great grace. How good of God to provide a path whereby our lives can be taken over by love and joy and peace and patience and kindness and goodness and faithfulness and gentleness and self-control.

RICHARD J. FOSTER

I love the LORD because he hears and answers my prayers. Because he bends down and listens, I will pray as long as I have breath!

PSALM 116:1–2 NLT

We can now come fearlessly into God's presence, assured of his glad welcome.

EPHESIANS 3:12 NLT

Delighting in Nature

What inexpressible joy for me, to look up through the apple blossoms and the fluttering leaves, and to see God's love there; to listen to the thrush that has built his nest among them, and to feel God's love, who cares for the birds, in every note that swells his little throat; to look beyond to the bright blue depths of the sky, and feel they are a canopy of blessing—the roof of the house of my Father.

ELIZABETH RUNDELL CHARLES

If we are children of God, we have a tremendous treasure in nature and will realize that it is holy and sacred. We will see God reaching out to us in every wind that blows, every sunrise and sunset, every cloud in the sky, every flower that blooms, and every leaf that fades.

OSWALD CHAMBERS

Look up at all the stars in the night sky
and hear your Father saying, "I carefully
set each one in its place. Know that I love
you more than these." Sit by the lake's
edge, listening to the water lapping the
shore, and hear your Father gently calling
you to that place near His heart.

*The heavens are telling the glory
of God; and the firmament
proclaims his handiwork.*

PSALM 19:1 NRSV

Someone Special

The Creator thinks enough of you to have sent
Someone very special so that you might have life—
abundantly, joyfully, completely, and victoriously.

When we love someone, we want to be with them,
and we view their love for us with great honor
even if they are not a person of great status.
For this reason—and not because of our great
status—God values our love. So much, in fact,
that He suffered greatly on our behalf.

JOHN CHRYSOSTOM

Everyone has a unique role to fill in the world and is
important in some respect. Everyone, including and
perhaps especially you, is indispensable.

NATHANIEL HAWTHORNE

One of Jesus' specialties is to make
somebodies out of nobodies.

Henrietta Mears

Every person ever created is so special that
their presence in the world makes it richer and
fuller and more wonderful than it could ever
have been without them.

God gives us all gifts, special abilities that we
are entrusted with developing to help serve
Him and serve others.

*God demonstrates His own love toward
us, in that while we were yet sinners,
Christ died for us.*

Romans 5:8 NASB

He Values Our Love

We are of such value to God that He came
to live among us…and to guide us home.
He will go to any length to seek us.… We can
only respond by loving God for His love.

CATHERINE OF SIENA

God loves us for ourselves. He values our love more
than He values galaxies of new created worlds.

A.W. TOZER

That is God's call to us—simply to be people
who are content to live close to Him and
to renew the kind of life in which the
closeness is felt and experienced.

THOMAS MERTON

We love him, because he first loved us.

1 JOHN 4:19 KJV

In our unquenchable longing to know God
personally, we pursue Him with passion and find
He is relentless in His pursuit of us.

*The God who made the world and everything
in it is the Lord of heaven and earth....
He himself gives all men life and breath
and everything else.... God did this so that
men would seek him and perhaps reach
out for him and find him, though he is not
far from each one of us. "For in him we live,
and move, and have our being."*

ACTS 17:24–25, 27–28 NIV

Showers of Blessings

God, who is love—who is, if I may say it
this way, made out of love—simply cannot
help but shed blessing on blessing upon us.

HANNAH WHITALL SMITH

There is plenitude in God....
God is a vast reservoir of blessing
who supplies us abundantly.

EUGENE PETERSON

God is above, presiding; beneath,
sustaining; within, filling.

HILDEBERT OF LAVARDIN

From the fullness of his grace we have all
received one blessing after another.

JOHN 1:16 NIV

However many blessings we expect
from God, His infinite liberality
will always exceed all our wishes
and our thoughts.

JOHN CALVIN

I lavish unfailing love for a thousand
generations on those who love me
and obey my commands.

EXODUS 20:6 NLT

*I will make a covenant of peace with them....
I will bless them.... I will send down showers
in season; there will be showers of blessing.*

EZEKIEL 34:25–26 NIV

The Beauty Within

All God's glory and beauty come from within, and there He delights to dwell. His visits there are frequent, His conversation sweet, His comforts refreshing, His peace passing all understanding.

THOMAS À KEMPIS

God's holy beauty comes near you, like a spiritual scent, and it stirs your drowsing soul.... He creates in you the desire to find Him and run after Him— to follow wherever He leads you, and to press peacefully against His heart wherever He is.

JOHN OF THE CROSS

God is within all things, but not included; outside all things, but not excluded, above all things, but not beyond their reach.

POPE ST. GREGORY I

Within each of us there is an inner place
where the living God himself longs to dwell,
our sacred center of belief.

Look deep within yourself and recognize
what brings life and grace into your heart....
You are loved by God.

CHRISTOPHER DE VINCK

I pray Thee, O God, that I may be beautiful within.

SOCRATES

And so we are transfigured…
our lives gradually becoming brighter
and more beautiful as God enters our
lives and we become like him.

2 CORINTHIANS 3:18 MSG

Promise of Love

A rainbow stretches from one end of the sky
to the other. Each shade of color, each facet of
light displays the radiant spectrum of God's
love: a promise that He will always love each
one of us at our worst and at our best.

Faithful, O Lord, Thy mercies are,
A rock that cannot move!
A thousand promises declare
Thy constancy of love.

CHARLES WESLEY

God's love never ceases. Never.... God doesn't
love us less if we fail or more if we succeed.
God's love never ceases.

MAX LUCADO

God promises to keep us in the palm of His
hand, with or without our awareness.
God has already made a space for us, even if
we have not made a space for God.

DAVID AND BARBARA SORENSEN

The steadfast love of the LORD never ceases,
his mercies never come to an end; they are new
every morning; great is your faithfulness.

LAMENTATIONS 3:22–23 NRSV

You are God's created beauty and the focus
of His affection and delight.

JANET L. WEAVER SMITH

GOD *promises to love me all day, sing songs*
all through the night! My life is God's prayer.

PSALM 42:8 MSG

Unconditional Love

God says, "I love you no matter what you do."
His love is unconditional and unending.

We are so preciously loved by God that we
cannot even comprehend it. No created being
can ever know how much and how sweetly and
tenderly God loves them. It is only with the
help of His grace that we are able to persevere
in…endless wonder at the high, surpassing,
immeasurable love which our Lord in His
goodness has for us.

Julian of Norwich

God loves you in the morning sun and the
evening rain, without caution or regret.

Brennan Manning

Do not dwell upon your inner failings.... Just do this: Bring your soul to the Great Physician—exactly as you are, even and especially at your worst moment.... For it is in such moments that you will most readily sense His healing presence.

TERESA OF AVILA

If you have a special need today, focus your full attention on the goodness and greatness of your Father rather than on the size of your need. Your need is so small compared to His ability to meet it.

I have loved you with an everlasting love;
I have drawn you with loving-kindness.

JEREMIAH 31:3 NIV

Watchful Care

He paints the lily of the field,
Perfumes each lily bell;
If He so loves the little flowers,
I know He loves me well.

MARIA STRAUS

God cares for the world He created, from
the rising of a nation to the falling of the
sparrow. Everything in the world lies under the
watchful gaze of His providential eyes, from
the numbering of the days of our life to the
numbering of the hairs on our head. When
we look at the world from that perspective, it
produces within us a response of reverence.

KEN GIRE

God's in His heaven—
All's right with the world!

ROBERT BROWNING

Let the morning bring me word of your unfailing
love, for I have put my trust in you.

PSALM 143:8 NIV

We do not understand the intricate pattern of the
stars in their courses, but we know that He who
created them does, and that just as surely as He
guides them, He is charting a safe course for us.

BILLY GRAHAM

*For He will give His angels charge concerning
you, to guard you in all your ways.*

PSALM 91:11 NASB

Our Sustaining Help

Source of my life's refreshing springs,
Whose presence in my heart sustains me,
Thy love ordains me pleasant things,
Thy mercy orders all that pains me.

A. L. Waring

We sometimes fear to bring our troubles to God,
because they must seem small to Him who sitteth
on the circle of the earth. But if they are large
enough to...endanger our welfare, they are large
enough to touch His heart of love.

R. A. Torrey

God...rekindles burned-out lives with fresh hope,
restoring dignity and respect to their lives—a place
in the sun!

1 Samuel 2:8 msg

Bless the LORD, O my soul,
And all that is within me, bless His holy name.
Bless the LORD, O my soul,
And forget none of His benefits;
Who pardons all your iniquities,
Who heals all your diseases;
Who redeems your life from the pit,
Who crowns you with
lovingkindness and compassion;
Who satisfies your years with good things,
So that your youth is renewed like the eagle.

PSALM 103:1–5 NASB

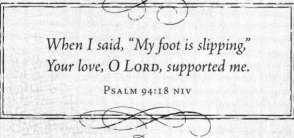

When I said, "My foot is slipping,"
Your love, O LORD, supported me.

PSALM 94:18 NIV

God Listens

Open wide the windows of our spirits
and fill us full of light; open wide the door
of our hearts, that we may receive and entertain
Thee with all our powers of adoration.

CHRISTINA ROSSETTI

We come this morning—
Like empty pitchers to a full fountain,
With no merits of our own,
O Lord—open up a window of heaven...
And listen this morning.

JAMES WELDON JOHNSON

God listens in compassion and love,
just like we do when our children come to us.
He delights in our presence.

RICHARD J. FOSTER

The heart speaks but a whispered prayer.
God hears and answers.

I have sought Thy nearness;
With all my heart have I called Thee,
And going out to meet Thee
I found Thee coming toward me.

Yehuda Halevi

Whatever the circumstances,
whatever the call…His strength will
be your strength in your hour of need.

Billy Graham

God knows the rhythm of your spirit and knows
your heart thoughts. He is as close as breathing.

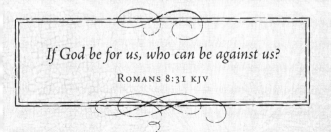

If God be for us, who can be against us?

Romans 8:31 kjv

A River of Delights

Your love, O LORD, reaches to the heavens, your
faithfulness to the skies. Your righteousness is
like the mighty mountains, your justice like the
great deep.... How priceless is your unfailing
love! Both high and low among men find refuge
in the shadow of your wings. They feast on the
abundance of your house; you give them drink
from your river of delights. For with you is the
fountain of life; in your light we see light.

PSALM 36:5–9 NIV

God's love is like a river springing up in the
Divine Substance and flowing endlessly through
His creation, filling all things with life and
goodness and strength.

THOMAS MERTON

As we grow in our capacities to see and enjoy
the joys that God has placed in our lives,
life becomes a glorious experience of
discovering His endless wonders.

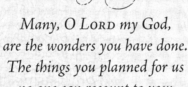

*Many, O LORD my God,
are the wonders you have done.
The things you planned for us
no one can recount to you;
were I to speak and tell of them,
they would be too many to declare.*

PSALM 40:5 NIV

Faithful Guide

God, who has led you safely on so far, will lead you
on to the end. Be altogether at rest in the loving
holy confidence which you ought to have
in His heavenly Providence.

FRANCIS DE SALES

Guidance is a sovereign act. Not merely does God
will to guide us by showing us His way...whatever
mistakes we may make, we shall come safely home.
Slippings and strayings there will be, no doubt, but
the everlasting arms are beneath us; we shall be
caught, rescued, restored. This is God's promise;
this is how good He is. And our self-distrust, while
keeping us humble, must not cloud the joy with
which we lean on our faithful covenant God.

J. I. PACKER

When we obey him, every path he guides us on is
fragrant with his lovingkindness and his truth.

PSALM 25:10 TLB

Heaven often seems distant and unknown,
but if he who made the road…is our guide,
we need not fear to lose the way.

HENRY VAN DYKE

*The LORD will guide you always; he will
satisfy your needs in a sun-scorched land....
You will be like a well-watered garden,
like a spring whose waters never fail.*

ISAIAH 58:11 NIV

Friendship with God

Friendship with God is a two-way street....
Jesus said that He tells His friends all that
His Father has told Him; close friends
communicate thoroughly and make
a transfer of heart and thought. How
awesome is our opportunity to be friends
with God, the almighty Creator of all!

BEVERLY LAHAYE

God's friendship is the unexpected joy we
find when we reach His outstretched hand.

JANET L. WEAVER SMITH

We can look to God as our Father. We can have a personal sense of His love for us and His interest in us, for He is concerned about us as a father is concerned for his children.... Incredible as it may seem, God wants our companionship. He wants to have us close to Him. He wants to be a father to us, to shield us, to protect us, to counsel us, and to guide us in our way through life.

BILLY GRAHAM

I have called you friends, for all things
that I have heard from My Father
I have made known to you.

JOHN 15:15 NASB

Divine Romance

To fall in love with God is the greatest of
all romances—to seek Him the greatest
of all adventures, to find Him the greatest
human achievement.

AUGUSTINE

In the morning let our hearts gaze upon
God's love...and in the beauty of that
vision, let us go forth to meet the day.

ROY LESSIN

Nothing in all creation will ever be able
to separate us from the love of God.

ROMANS 8:39 NLT

Love Him totally who gave Himself
totally for your love.

CLARE OF ASSISI

Before anything else, above all else, beyond everything
else, God loves us. God loves us extravagantly,
ridiculously, without limit or condition.
God is in love with us…God yearns for us.

ROBERTA BONDI

The love of God is broader
than the measure of our mind
And the heart of the Eternal
is most wonderfully kind.

FREDERICK W. FABER

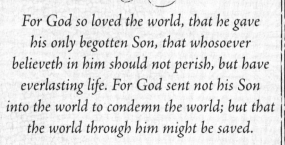

*For God so loved the world, that he gave
his only begotten Son, that whosoever
believeth in him should not perish, but have
everlasting life. For God sent not his Son
into the world to condemn the world; but that
the world through him might be saved.*

JOHN 3:16–17 KJV

Joy Is...

Joy is the touch of God's finger. The object of our longing is not the touch but the Toucher. This is true of all good things—they are all God's touch. Whatever we desire, we are really desiring God.

PETER KREEFT

Joy is really a road sign pointing us to God. Once we have found God...we no longer need to trouble ourselves so much about the quest for joy.

C. S. LEWIS

The love of the Father is like a sudden rain shower that will pour forth when you least expect it, catching you up into wonder and praise.

RICHARD J. FOSTER

It is God's knowledge of me, His careful
husbanding of the ground of my being,
His constant presence in the garden of my
little life that guarantees my joy.

W. PHILLIP KELLER

Joy is the echo of God's life within us.

*So be truly glad. There is wonderful joy
ahead.... You love him even though you
have never seen him. Though you do not
see him now, you trust him; and you rejoice
with a glorious, inexpressible joy.*

1 PETER 1:6, 8–9 NLT

Glorious Handiwork

He made you so you could share in His creation,
could love and laugh and know Him.

TED GRIFFEN

The whole earth is full of his glory.

ISAIAH 6:3 KJV

The huge dome of the sky is of all things sensuously
perceived the most like infinity. When God made
space and worlds that move in space, and clothed
our world with air, and gave us such eyes and such
imaginations as those we have, He knew what the
sky would mean to us.... We cannot be certain that
this was not indeed one of the chief purposes for
which Nature was created.

C. S. LEWIS

You are a creation of God unequaled anywhere in
the universe.... Thank Him for yourself and then
for all the rest of His glorious handiwork.

Norman Vincent Peale

The LORD is my strength and my song;
he has become my salvation.
He is my God, and I will praise him,
my father's God, and I will exalt him....
Who is like you—majestic in holiness,
awesome in glory, working wonders?

Exodus 15:2, 11 NIV

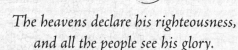

The heavens declare his righteousness,
and all the people see his glory.

Psalm 97:6 KJV

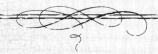

Countless Beauties

From the world we see, hear, and touch,
we behold inspired visions that reveal God's glory.
In the sun's light, we catch warm rays of grace
and glimpse His eternal design. In the birds' song,
we hear His voice and it reawakens our desire
for Him. At the wind's touch, we feel His Spirit
and sense our eternal existence.

WENDY MOORE

Though I have seen the oceans and mountains,
though I have read great books and seen great
works of art, though I have heard symphonies and
tasted the best wines and foods,.there is nothing
greater or more beautiful than those people I love.

CHRISTOPHER DE VINCK

Try to see the beauty "in your own backyard,"
to notice the miracles of everyday life, to see the
specialness of your own children and to value the
treasure of a good marriage.

GLORIA GAITHER

Not every day of our lives is overflowing with joy
and celebration. But there are moments when our
hearts nearly burst within us for the sheer joy of
being alive. The first sight of our newborn babies,
the warmth of love in another's eyes, the fresh scent
of rain on a hot summer's eve—moments like these
renew in us a heartfelt appreciation for life.

GWEN ELLIS

Worship the LORD in the beauty of holiness.

PSALM 96:9 KJV

Love without Limits

Everything which relates to God is infinite. We must therefore, while we keep our hearts humble, keep our aims high. Our highest services are indeed but finite, imperfect. But as God is unlimited in goodness, He should have our unlimited love.

HANNAH MORE

There is no limit to God's love. It is without measure and its depth cannot be sounded.

MOTHER TERESA

Your roots will grow down into God's love and keep you strong. And may you have the power to understand, as all God's people should, how wide, how long, how high, and how deep his love is.

EPHESIANS 3:17–18 NLT

Could we with ink the ocean fill,
And were the skies of parchment made,
Were every stalk on earth a quill,
And every man a scribe by trade
To write the love of God above
Would drain the ocean dry,
Nor could the scroll contain the whole
Though stretched from sky to sky.

MEIR BEN ISAAC NEHORAI

God's love is meteoric, his loyalty astronomic,
His purpose titanic, his verdicts oceanic.
Yet in his largeness nothing gets lost.

PSALM 36:5–6 MSG

A Quiet Sanctuary

Deep within us all there is an amazing inner
sanctuary of the soul, a holy place...to which we
may continuously return. Eternity is at our hearts,
pressing upon our time-torn lives, warming us...
calling us home unto Itself. Yielding to these
persuasions...utterly and completely, to the Light
within, is the beginning of true life.... Life from
the Center is a life of unhurried peace, and power.
It is simple. It is serene.... We need not get frantic.
He is at the helm. And when our little day is done
we lie down quietly in peace, for all is well.

THOMAS R. KELLY

Don't get so busy that you miss the beauty of a day
or the serenity of a quiet moment alone. For it is
often life's smallest pleasures and gentlest joys that
make the biggest and most lasting difference.

You are valuable just because you exist. Not because
of what you do or what you have done, but simply
because you are. Just think about the way Jesus
honors you...and smile.

MAX LUCADO

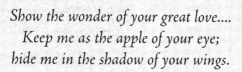

Show the wonder of your great love....
Keep me as the apple of your eye;
hide me in the shadow of your wings.

PSALM 17:7–8 NIV

Always There

We need never shout across the spaces to an absent God. He is nearer than our own soul, closer than our most secret thoughts.

A. W. TOZER

God is always present in the temple of your heart... His home. And when you come in to meet Him there, you find that it is the one place of deep satisfaction where every longing is met.

Always be in a state of expectancy, and see that you leave room for God to come in as He likes.

OSWALD CHAMBERS

God is steadfast as your rock, faithful as your protector, sleepless as your watcher.

God is the God of promise. He keeps His word,
even when that seems impossible.

COLIN URQUHART

We have a Father in heaven who is almighty, who
loves His children as He loves His only-begotten
Son, and whose very joy and delight it is to...help
them at all times and under all circumstances.

GEORGE MÜLLER

*The LORD your God will personally
go ahead of you. He will neither
fail you nor abandon you.*

DEUTERONOMY 31:6 NLT

Sought and Found

It is God's will that we believe that we see Him continually, though it seems to us that the sight be only partial; and through this belief He makes us always to gain more grace, for God wishes to be seen, and He wishes to be sought, and He wishes to be expected, and He wishes to be trusted.

Julian of Norwich

To seek God means first of all to let yourself be found by Him.

God's nature is given me. His love is jealous for my life. All His attributes are woven into the pattern of my spirit. What a God is this! His life implanted in every child. Thank you, Father, for this.

Jim Elliot

In the deepest heart of everyone, God planted a
longing for Himself as He is: a God of love.

EUGENIA PRICE

To them that seek Thee thou art good,
To them that find Thee, all in all.

BERNARD OF CLAIRVAUX

Your beauty and love chase after
me every day of my life.

PSALM 23:6 MSG

*If you search for him with all your
heart and soul, you will find him.*

DEUTERONOMY 4:29 NLT

The Majesty of God

O Lord, our Lord, how majestic is your name in
all the earth! You have set your glory above the
heavens.... When I consider your heavens, the work
of your fingers, the moon and the stars, which you
have set in place, what is man that you are mindful
of him, the son of man that you care for him?...
How majestic is your name in all the earth!

Psalm 8:1–4, 9 niv

Savor little glimpses of God's goodness
and His majesty, thankful for the gift of them.

For God is, indeed, a wonderful Father
who longs to pour out His mercy upon us,
and whose majesty is so great that He can
transform us from deep within.

Teresa of Avila

Search high and low, scan skies and land,
you'll find nothing and no one quite like GOD.
The holy angels are in awe before him; he looms
immense and august over everyone around
him. GOD-of-the-Angel-Armies, who is like you,
powerful and faithful from every angle?

PSALM 89:6–8 MSG

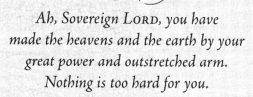

*Ah, Sovereign LORD, you have
made the heavens and the earth by your
great power and outstretched arm.
Nothing is too hard for you.*

JEREMIAH 32:17 NIV

Designed on Purpose

It's in Christ that we find out who we are and
what we are living for. Long before we first
heard of Christ and got our hopes up, he had
his eye on us, had designs on us for glorious
living, part of the overall purpose he is working
out in everything and everyone.

EPHESIANS 1:11–12 MSG

To every thing there is a season, and a time
to every purpose under the heaven.

ECCLESIASTES 3:1 KJV

All the days ordained for me were written
in your book before one of them came to be.

PSALM 139:16 NIV

Every person's life is a fairy tale written
by God's fingers.

Hans Christian Andersen

Remember the things I have done in the past.
For I alone am God!
I am God, and there is none like me.
Only I can tell you the future
before it even happens.
Everything I plan will come to pass.

Isaiah 46:9–10 nlt

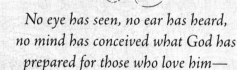

No eye has seen, no ear has heard,
no mind has conceived what God has
prepared for those who love him—
but God has revealed it to us by his Spirit.

1 Corinthians 2:9–10 niv

Restoration

The Lord promises to bind up the brokenhearted,
to give relief and full deliverance to those whose
spirits have been weighed down.

CHARLES R. SWINDOLL

Our hunger for significance is a signal
of who we are and why we are here, and it also is
the basis of humanity's enduring response to Jesus.
For He always takes individual human beings
as seriously as their shredded dignity demands,
and He has the resources to carry through
with His high estimate of them.

DALLAS WILLARD

Ye fearful saints fresh courage take
The clouds you so much dread
Are big with mercy and shall break
With blessings on your head.

WILLIAM COWPER

It is God who arms me with strength,
And makes my way perfect.
He makes my feet like the feet of deer,
And sets me on my high places....
You have also given me the shield of Your salvation;
Your right hand has held me up,
Your gentleness has made me great.
You enlarged my path under me,
So my feet did not slip.

PSALM 18:32–33, 35–36 NKJV

But those who hope in the LORD will renew
their strength. They will soar on wings
like eagles; they will run and not grow weary,
they will walk and not be faint.

ISAIAH 40:31 NIV

See How He Loves Us

Go outside, to the fields, enjoy nature and the sunshine, go out and try to recapture happiness in yourself and in God. Think of all the beauty that's still left in and around you and be happy!

ANNE FRANK

The beauty of the earth, the beauty of the sky, the order of the stars, the sun, the moon…their very loveliness is their confession of God: for who made these lovely mutable things, but He who is himself unchangeable beauty?

AUGUSTINE

O God, creator of light: at the rising of Your sun this morning, let the greatest of all lights, Your love, rise like the sun within our hearts.

ARMENIAN APOSTOLIC CHURCH

Blue skies with white clouds on summer days.
A myriad of stars on clear moonlit nights. Tulips
and roses and violets and dandelions and daisies.
Bluebirds and laughter and sunshine and Easter.
See how He loves us!

ALICE CHAPIN

His tenderness in the springing grass,
His beauty in the flowers,
His living love in the sun above—
All here, and near, and ours.

CHARLOTTE PERKINS GILMAN

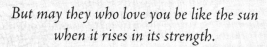

*But may they who love you be like the sun
when it rises in its strength.*

JUDGES 5:31 NIV

Surrounded by Love

The light of God surrounds me,
The love of God enfolds me,
The presence of God watches over me,
Wherever I am, God is.

He is everything that is good and comfortable
for us. He is our clothing that for love wraps us,
clasps us, and all surrounds us for tender love.

JULIAN OF NORWICH

In God's wisdom, He frequently chooses to meet
our needs by showing His love toward us through
the hands and hearts of others.

JACK HAYFORD

The LORD is my strength and my shield;
my heart trusted in him, and I am helped.

PSALM 28:7 KJV

The Lord's goodness surrounds us at every
moment. I walk through it almost with difficulty,
as through thick grass and flowers.

R. W. Barber

Love is the sweet, tender, melting nature
of God flowing into the creature, making
the creature most like unto Himself.

Isaac Penington

What can harm us when everything must first
touch God whose presence surrounds us?

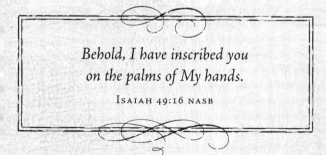

*Behold, I have inscribed you
on the palms of My hands.*

Isaiah 49:16 nasb

The Grace of God

But God, being rich in mercy, because of His great love with which He loved us, even when we were dead in our transgressions, made us alive together with Christ (by grace you have been saved), and raised us up with Him, and seated us with Him in the heavenly places in Christ Jesus, so that in the ages to come He might show the surpassing riches of His grace in kindness toward us in Christ Jesus. For by grace you have been saved through faith; and that not of yourselves, it is the gift of God; not as a result of works, so that no one may boast. For we are His workmanship, created in Christ Jesus for good works, which God prepared beforehand so that we would walk in them.

Ephesians 2:4–10 nasb

Grace means that God already loves us
as much as an infinite God can possibly love.

PHILIP YANCEY

God's forgiveness and love exist for you
as if you were the only person on earth.

CECIL OSBORNE

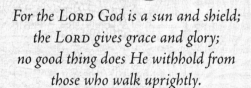

For the LORD God is a sun and shield;
the LORD gives grace and glory;
no good thing does He withhold from
those who walk uprightly.

PSALM 84:11 NASB

The Faithfulness of God

The Lord is righteous.... He will do no injustice.
Every morning He brings His justice to light;
He does not fail.

ZEPHANIAH 3:5 NASB

It is good to give thanks to the Lord and to
sing praises to Your name, O Most High;
to declare Your lovingkindness in the morning
and Your faithfulness by night.

PSALM 92:1–2 NASB

God takes care of His own.... At just the right
moment He steps in and proves Himself
as our faithful heavenly Father.

CHARLES R. SWINDOLL

And the God of love and peace shall be with you.

2 CORINTHIANS 13:11 KJV

Be assured, if you walk with Him and look to Him
and expect help from Him, He will never fail you.

GEORGE MÜLLER

I will sing of the mercies of the LORD for ever:
with my mouth will I make known
thy faithfulness to all generations.

PSALM 89:1 KJV

*For your unfailing love is as high
as the heavens. Your faithfulness reaches
to the clouds. Be exalted, O God, above
the highest heavens. May your glory
shine over all the earth.*

PSALM 57:10–11 NLT

The Promise of Rest

The promise of "arrival" and "rest" is still there
for God's people. God himself is at rest.
And at the end of the journey we'll surely
rest with God. So let's keep at it and eventually
arrive at the place of rest.

HEBREWS 4:9–11 MSG

Come unto me, all ye that labour and are heavy
laden, and I will give you rest. Take my yoke
upon you, and learn of me; for I am meek and
lowly in heart: and ye shall find rest unto your
souls. For my yoke is easy, and my burden is light.

MATTHEW 11:28–30 KJV

In His arms He carries us all day long.

FANNY J. CROSBY

The same God who guides the stars in their courses, who directs the earth in its orbit, who feeds the burning furnace of the sun, and keeps the stars perpetually burning with their fires—the same God has promised to supply thy strength.

CHARLES SPURGEON

When God finds a soul that rests in Him and is not easily moved...to this same soul He gives the joy of His presence.

CATHERINE OF GENOA

My Presence will go with you, and I will give you rest.

EXODUS 33:14 NIV

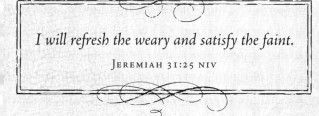

I will refresh the weary and satisfy the faint.

JEREMIAH 31:25 NIV

Tender Love

God's fingers can touch nothing but
to mold it into loveliness.

George MacDonald

He has remembered his love and his
faithfulness...all the ends of the earth have
seen the salvation of our God.

Psalm 98:3 niv

You who have received so much love share
it with others. Love others the way that
God has loved you, with tenderness.

Mother Teresa

Lord, don't hold back your tender mercies
from me. My only hope is in your unfailing
love and faithfulness.

Psalm 40:11 nlt

Love is a great thing. By itself it makes
everything that is heavy light;
and it bears evenly all that is uneven.

THOMAS À KEMPIS

You, O God, are both tender and kind, not easily
angered, immense in love, and you never, never quit.

PSALM 86:15 MSG

For all God's words are right,
and everything he does is worthy of our trust.
He loves whatever is just and good;
the earth is filled with his tender love.

PSALM 33:4–5 TLB

Source of Wonder

The longer I live, the more my mind dwells upon
the beauty and the wonder of the world.

John Burroughs

I would maintain that thanks are the highest
form of thought, and that gratitude
is happiness doubled by wonder.

G. K. Chesterton

Dear Lord, grant me the grace of wonder.
Surprise me, amaze me, awe me in every
crevice of your universe.... Each day enrapture
me with your marvelous things without number.
I do not ask to see the reason for it all;
I ask only to share the wonder of it all.

Joshua Abraham Heschel

May our lives be illumined
by the steady radiance
renewed daily,
of a wonder,
the source of which
is beyond reason.

<small>DAG HAMMARSKJÖLD</small>

Our Creator would never have made such
lovely days, and have given us the deep hearts
to enjoy them, above and beyond all thought,
unless we were meant to be immortal.

<small>NATHANIEL HAWTHORNE</small>

*I will give thanks to the LORD with all
my heart; I will tell of all Your wonders.
I will be glad and exult in You; I will sing
praise to Your name, O Most High.*

<small>PSALM 9:1–2 NASB</small>

Full Protection

But let all who take refuge in you be glad; let them
ever sing for joy. Spread your protection over them,
that those who love your name may rejoice in you.
For surely, O LORD, you bless the righteous; you
surround them with your favor as with a shield.

PSALM 5:11–12 NIV

Lord, the task is impossible for me but not
for Thee. Lead the way and I will follow.
Why should I fear? I am on a royal mission.
I am in the service of the King of kings.

MARY SLESSOR

Leave behind your fear and dwell on the
lovingkindness of God, that you may
recover by gazing on Him.

By my power I will make my people strong,
and by my authority they will go wherever they
wish. I, the Lord, have spoken!

ZECHARIAH 10:12 NLT

How great is the goodness you have stored up
for those who fear you. You lavish it on those
who come to you for protection,
blessing them before the watching world.

PSALM 31:19 NLT

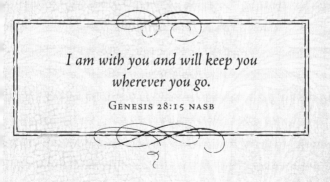

*I am with you and will keep you
wherever you go.*

GENESIS 28:15 NASB

Unfailing Love

Give thanks to the LORD, for he is good!
His faithful love endures forever.

PSALM 136:1 NLT

God is not only the answer to a thousand needs,
He is the answer to a thousand wants. He is the
fulfillment of our chief desire in all of life. For
whether or not we've ever recognized it, what
we desire is unfailing love. Oh, God, awake our
souls to see—You are what we want, not just
what we need. Yes, our life's protection, but also
our heart's affection. Yes, our soul's salvation,
but also our heart's exhilaration. Unfailing love.
A love that will not let me go!

BETH MOORE

The greatest honor we can give God is to live
gladly because of the knowledge of His love.

JULIAN OF NORWICH

The loving God we serve has immeasurable
compassion and tenderness toward each of us
throughout our lives.

JAMES DOBSON

What good news! God knows me completely
and still loves me.

*Satisfy us in the morning with your
unfailing love, that we may sing
for joy and be glad all our days.*

PSALM 90:14 NIV

Enfolded in Peace

I will let God's peace infuse every part of today. As the chaos swirls and life's demands pull at me on all sides, I will breathe in God's peace that surpasses all understanding. He has promised that He would set within me a peace too deeply planted to be affected by unexpected or exhausting demands.

WENDY MOORE

Calm me, O Lord, as you stilled the storm,
Still me, O Lord, keep me from harm.
Let all the tumult within me cease,
Enfold me, Lord, in your peace.

CELTIC TRADITIONAL

Love comes while we rest against our Father's chest.
Joy comes when we catch the rhythms of His heart.
Peace comes when we live in harmony
with those rhythms.

KEN GIRE

Drop Thy still dews of quietness,
Till all our strivings cease;
Take from our souls the strain and stress,
And let our ordered lives confess
The beauty of Thy peace.

JOHN GREENLEAF WHITTIER

Because of the tender mercy of our God, with which the Sunrise from on high will visit us, to shine upon those who sit in darkness…to guide our feet into the way of peace.

LUKE 1:78–79 NASB

God's Compassion

Through the LORD's mercies we are not consumed,
Because His compassions fail not.
They are new every morning;
Great is Your faithfulness.
"The LORD is my portion," says my soul,
Therefore I hope in Him!"
The LORD is good to those who wait for Him,
To the soul who seeks Him....
For the Lord will not cast off forever.
Though He causes grief,
Yet He will show compassion
According to the multitude of His mercies.

LAMENTATIONS 3:22–25, 31–32 NKJV

Be kind and compassionate to one another,
forgiving each other, just as in Christ
God forgave you.

EPHESIANS 4:32 NIV

The compassionate person feels with God's heart.

In His love He clothes us, enfolds us,
and embraces us; that tender love completely
surrounds us, never to leave us.

JULIAN OF NORWICH

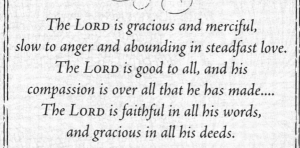

*The LORD is gracious and merciful,
slow to anger and abounding in steadfast love.
The LORD is good to all, and his
compassion is over all that he has made....
The LORD is faithful in all his words,
and gracious in all his deeds.*

PSALM 145:8–9, 13 NRSV

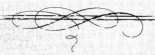

Fear Not

Don't be afraid, I've redeemed you. I've called
your name. You're mine. When you're in over
your head, I'll be there with you. When you're in
rough waters, you will not go down. When you're
between a rock and a hard place, it won't be a
dead end—Because I am God, your personal
God, The Holy of Israel, your Savior. I paid a
huge price for you...! That's how much you mean
to me! That's how much I love you!

ISAIAH 43:1–4 MSG

Do not be afraid to enter the cloud that is
settling down on your life. God is in it.
The other side is radiant with His glory.

L. B. COWMAN

In the multitude of my anxieties within me,
Your comforts delight my soul.

PSALM 94:19 NKJV

Grasp the fact that God is for you…. You will
find in thus knowing God as your sovereign
protector, irrevocably committed to you
in the covenant of grace, both freedom from
fear and new strength for the fight.

J. I. PACKER

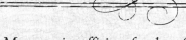

*My grace is sufficient for thee: for my strength
is made perfect in weakness.*

2 CORINTHIANS 12:9 KJV

Holy and Whole

May God himself, the God who makes everything
holy and whole, make you holy and whole, put you
together—spirit, soul, and body—and keep you
fit for the coming of our Master, Jesus Christ. The
One who called you is completely dependable.

1 Thessalonians 5:23–24 MSG

He has made everything beautiful in its time.

Ecclesiastes 3:11 NIV

God is every moment totally aware
of each one of us. Totally aware in intense
concentration and love.... No one passes
through any area of life, happy or tragic,
without the attention of God with him.

Eugenia Price

Because God is responsible for our welfare, we are
told to cast all our care upon Him, for He cares for
us. God says, "I'll take the burden—don't give it a
thought—leave it to Me." God is keenly aware that
we are dependent upon Him for life's necessities.

BILLY GRAHAM

*So spacious is he, so roomy, that everything
of God finds its proper place in him without
crowding. Not only that, but all the broken
and dislocated pieces of the universe—people
and things, animals and atoms—get properly
fixed and fit together in vibrant harmonies.*

COLOSSIANS 1:19–20 MSG

A Spirit of Hope

Hope, like the gleaming taper's light,
Adorns and cheers our way;
And still, as darker grows the night,
Emits a brighter ray.

OLIVER GOLDSMITH

I pray also that the eyes of your heart may
be enlightened in order that you may know the
hope to which he has called you.

EPHESIANS 1:18 NIV

Hope floods my heart with delight!
Running on air, mad with life, dizzy, reeling,
Upward I mount—faith is sight, life is feeling,
Hope is the day-star of might!

MARGARET WITTER FULLER

Hope sees the invisible, feels the intangible,
and achieves the impossible.

Let us draw near to God with a sincere
heart in full assurance of faith.... Let us hold
unswervingly to the hope we profess,
for he who promised is faithful.

Hebrews 10:22–23 niv

Because You live, O Christ,
the spirit bird of hope is freed for flying,
our cages of despair no longer keep us
closed and life-denying.

Shirley Erena Murray

If you do not hope, you will not find
what is beyond your hopes.

St. Clement of Alexandria

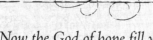

*Now the God of hope fill you with
all joy and peace in believing.*

Romans 15:13 kjv

Every Need

God wants nothing from us except our needs,
and these furnish Him with room to display
His bounty when He supplies them freely....
Not what I have, but what I do not have, is the
first point of contact between my soul and God.

CHARLES H. SPURGEON

Jesus Christ has brought every need,
every joy, every gratitude, every hope of
ours before God. He accompanies us
and brings us into the presence of God.

DIETRICH BONHOEFFER

The "air" which our souls need also envelops
all of us at all times and on all sides.
God is round about us...on every hand,
with many-sided and all-sufficient grace.

OLE HALLESBY

Are not five sparrows sold for two pennies? Yet not one of them is forgotten by God. Indeed, the very hairs of your head are all numbered. Don't be afraid; you are worth more than many sparrows.

LUKE 12:6–7 NIV

Where there is faith, there is love.
Where there is love, there is peace.
Where there is peace, there is God.
Where there is God, there is no need.

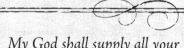

My God shall supply all your need according to his riches in glory by Christ Jesus.

PHILIPPIANS 4:19 KJV

Constancy

Dear Lord, today I thought of the words of Vincent
Van Gogh, "It is true that there is an ebb and
flow, but the sea remains the sea." You are the sea.
Although I may experience many ups and downs in
my emotions and often feel great shifts in my inner
life, You remain the same.... There are days
of sadness and days of joy; there are feelings of
guilt and feelings of gratitude; there are moments
of failure and moments of success; but all of them
are embraced by Your unwavering love.
My only real temptation is to doubt Your love...
to remove myself from the healing radiance
of Your love. To do these things is to move
into the darkness of despair.
O Lord, sea of love and goodness, let me not
fear too much the storms and winds of my daily life,
and let me know that there is ebb and flow...
but that the sea remains the sea.
Amen.

Henri J. M. Nouwen

For I am the LORD, I change not.

MALACHI 3:6 KJV

...The God who gives rain in both spring and
autumn and maintains the rhythm of the seasons....

JEREMIAH 5:24 MSG

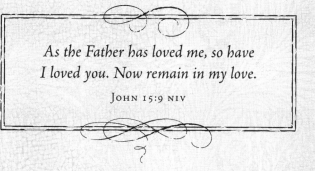

*As the Father has loved me, so have
I loved you. Now remain in my love.*

JOHN 15:9 NIV

You Are Valued!

A speaker held up a twenty-dollar bill and asked, "Who would like this twenty-dollar bill?" Hands shot up all around the room. He crumpled the bill, dropped it on the ground, and ground it into the floor with his heel. Picking it up, he asked, "Now who wants it?" Hands still went up. No matter what was done to the money, it was still desirable because it did not decrease in value. Many times in life, you will be dropped, crumpled, or ground into the dirt by your circumstances or the decisions you make. You may feel worthless and useless. But you will never lose your value. Dirty or clean, crumpled or finely creased, you are still priceless to those who love you and to the One who made you.

The value of a person is not measured on an
applause meter; it is measured in the heart
and mind of God.... Rest assured, for on God's
scale, the needle always reads high.

JOHN FISCHER

The LORD your God is with you,
he is mighty to save.
He will take great delight in you,
he will quiet you with his love,
he will rejoice over you with singing.

ZEPHANIAH 3:17 NIV

Settled in Solitude

Solitude liberates us from entanglements by carving
out a space from which we can see ourselves and
our situation before the Audience of One. Solitude
provides the private place where we can take our
bearings and so make God our North Star.

Os Guinness

Settle yourself in solitude and you
will come upon Him in yourself.

Teresa of Avila

We must drink deeply from the very Source the
deep calm and peace of interior quietude and
refreshment of God, allowing the pure water of
divine grace to flow plentifully and unceasingly
from the Source itself.

Mother Teresa

When I am with God my fear is gone; in the great
quiet of God my troubles are as the pebbles on the
road, my joys are like the everlasting hills.

WALTER RAUSCHENBUSCH

Be simple; take our Lord's hand
and walk through things.

FATHER ANDREW

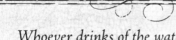

*Whoever drinks of the water that I will
give him shall never thirst; but the water that
I will give him will become in him a well
of water springing up to eternal life.*

JOHN 4:13–14 NASB

Destiny

Recognizing who we are in Christ and aligning
our life with God's purpose for us gives a sense of
destiny.... It gives form and direction to our life.

JEAN FLEMING

When we live life centered around what others like,
feel, and say, we lose touch with our own identity.
I am an eternal being, created by God. I am an
individual with purpose. It's not what I get from life,
but who I am, that makes the difference.

NEVA COYLE

God has a purpose for your life,
and no one else can take your place.

The patterns of our days are always rearranging...
and each design for living is unique,
graced with its own special beauty.

Happiness is living by inner purpose,
not by outer pressures.

DAVID AUGSBERGER

I believe that nothing that happens to me is
meaningless, and that it is good for us all that it
should be so, even if it runs counter to our own
wishes. As I see it, I'm here for some purpose,
and I only hope I may fulfill it.

DIETRICH BONHOEFFER

*May the favor of the Lord our God rest upon
us; establish the work of our hands for us.*

PSALM 90:17 NIV

For Himself

Although it be good to think upon the kindness of
God, and to love Him and worship Him for it; yet
it is far better to gaze upon the pure essence of Him
and to love Him and worship Him for Himself.

The reason for loving God is God Himself,
and the measure in which we should love Him
is to love Him without measure.

BERNARD OF CLAIRVAUX

We desire many things, and God offers us only one
thing. He can offer us only one thing—Himself.
He has nothing else to give.
There is nothing else to give.

PETER KREEFT

By love alone is God enjoyed; by love alone
delighted in, by love alone approached and admired.
His nature requires love.

THOMAS TRAHERNE

Love does not allow lovers
to belong anymore to themselves,
but they belong only to the Beloved.

DIONYSIUS

Love the LORD your God with all your heart,
all your soul, and all your strength.

DEUTERONOMY 6:5 NLT

*Know that the LORD Himself is God....We
are His people and the sheep of His pasture.*

PSALM 100:3 NASB

Lavish Gift-Giving

How blessed is God! And what a blessing
he is! He's the Father of our Master, Jesus
Christ, and takes us to the high places of
blessing in him. Long before he laid down
earth's foundations, he had us in mind, had
settled on us as the focus of his love, to be
made whole and holy by his love. Long, long
ago he decided to adopt us into his family
through Jesus Christ. (What pleasure he
took in planning this!) He wanted us to enter
into the celebration of his lavish gift-giving
by the hand of his beloved Son.

EPHESIANS 1:3–6 MSG

God loves us; not because we are lovable but because He is love, not because He needs to receive but because He delights to give.

C. S. Lewis

The impetus of God's love comes from within Himself, to share with us His life and love. It is a beautiful, eternal gift, held out to us in the hands of love. All we have to do is say "Yes!"

John Powell, S.J.

Every good gift and every perfect gift is from above, and comes down from the Father of lights, with whom there is no variation or shadow of turning.

James 1:17 nkjv

Path of Life

The path of the righteous is like the light of dawn,
that shines brighter and brighter until the full day.

PROVERBS 4:18 NASB

If by a still, small voice He calls
To paths I do not know,
I'll answer, dear Lord, with my hand in Yours,
I'll go where You want me to go.

MARY BROWN

Stay focused on God's ways and principles. Live
every day in the knowledge that He loves you
and He is present within you, enabling you to do
mighty things for His kingdom.

GEORGE BARNA

Thy word is a lamp unto my feet,
and a light unto my path.

PSALM 119:105 KJV

The way of Christ is not possible without Christ.

WILLIAM RUSSELL MALTBY

Come, and let us go up to the mountain of the
LORD...and he will teach us of his ways,
and we will walk in his paths.

MICAH 4:2 KJV

The best things are nearest...light in your eyes,
flowers at your feet, duties at your hand,
the path of God just before you.

ROBERT LOUIS STEVENSON

*You have made known to me the paths of life;
you will fill me with joy in your presence.*

ACTS 2:28 NIV

Nothing but Grace

There is nothing but God's grace. We walk upon it;
we breathe it; we live and die by it;
it makes the nails and axles of the universe.

ROBERT LOUIS STEVENSON

Grace is no stationary thing, it is ever becoming. It
is flowing straight out of God's heart. Grace does
nothing but re-form and convey God. Grace makes
the soul conformable to the will of God. God, the
ground of the soul, and grace go together.

MEISTER ECKHART

God is sheer mercy and grace; not easily angered,
he's rich in love.... As far as sunrise is from sunset,
he has separated us from our sins.

PSALM 103:8, 12 MSG

To be grateful is to recognize the Love of God in everything He has given us—and He has given us everything. Every breath we draw is a gift of His love, every moment of existence is a gift of grace.

THOMAS MERTON

And God is able to make all grace abound to you, so that in all things at all times, having all that you need, you will abound in every good work.

2 CORINTHIANS 9:8 NIV

Jars of Clay

But thanks be to God, who always leads
us in triumphal procession in Christ and
through us spreads everywhere the fragrance
of the knowledge of him. For we are to God
the aroma of Christ among those who are
being saved and those who are perishing.

2 CORINTHIANS 2:14–15 NIV

Our gifts and attainments are not only to be light
and warmth in our own dwellings, but are also to
shine through the windows into the dark night, to
guide and cheer bewildered travelers on the road.

HENRY WARD BEECHER

The deepest darkness is outshone
by the light of Jesus.

CORRIE TEN BOOM

Above all, believe confidently that Jesus
delights in maintaining that new
nature within you, and imparting to
it his strength and wisdom for its work.

ANDREW MURRAY

Lord, help me to spread Your fragrance
everywhere I go, and may Your radiant
light be visible through me.

*For God, who said, "Let light shine
out of darkness," made his light shine
in our hearts to give us the light of the
knowledge of the glory of God in the face
of Christ. But we have this treasure in jars
of clay to show that this all-surpassing
power is from God and not from us.*

2 CORINTHIANS 4:6–7 NIV

Go Out in Joy

You'll go out in joy, you'll be led into a whole
and complete life. The mountains and hills
will lead the parade, bursting with song.
All the trees of the forest will join the procession,
exuberant with applause.

ISAIAH 55:12 MSG

Sometimes our thoughts turn back toward
a corner in a forest, or the end of a bank,
or an orchard powdered with flowers, seen but a
single time...yet remaining in our hearts
and leaving in soul and body an unappeased
desire which is not to be forgotten, a feeling
we have just rubbed elbows with happiness.

GUY DE MAUPASSANT

You will fill me with joy in your presence,
with eternal pleasures at your right hand.

PSALM 16:11 NIV

Does not all nature around me praise God? If I were silent, I should be an exception to the universe. Does not the thunder praise Him as it rolls like drums in the march of the God of armies? Do not the mountains praise Him when the woods upon their summits wave in adoration? Does not the lightning write His name in letters of fire? Has not the whole earth a voice? And...can I silent be?

C. H. SPURGEON

He will once again fill your mouth with laughter and your lips with shouts of joy.

JOB 8:21 NLT

A Personal Guide

But I'll take the hand of those who don't
know the way, who can't see where they're going.
I'll be a personal guide to them, directing them
through unknown country. I'll be right there
to show them what roads to take, make sure
they don't fall into the ditch. These are
the things I'll be doing for them—sticking with
them, not leaving them for a minute.

ISAIAH 42:16 MSG

Who brought me hither will bring
me hence; no other guide I seek.

JOHN MILTON

We can make our plans, but the LORD
determines our steps.

PROVERBS 16:9 NLT

Abraham did not know the way,
but he knew the Guide.

LEE ROBERSON

Imagine what Israel and all of us who
worship Israel's God would have missed
if they had gone by the short route—the thrilling
story of the deliverance from Egypt's chariots
when the sea was rolled back. Let's not ask for
shortcuts. Let's keep alert for the wonders our
Guide will show us in the wilderness.

ELISABETH ELLIOT

Whether you turn to the right or to the left,
your ears will hear a voice behind you, saying,
"This is the way; walk in it."

ISAIAH 30:21 NIV

I Will Carry You

I will lift up my eyes to the hills—
From whence comes my help?
My help comes from the LORD,
Who made heaven and earth.
He will not allow your foot to be moved;
He who keeps you will not slumber.
Behold, He who keeps Israel
Shall neither slumber nor sleep.
The LORD is your keeper;
The LORD is your shade at your right hand.
The sun shall not strike you by day,
Nor the moon by night.
The LORD shall preserve you from all evil;
He shall preserve your soul.
The LORD shall preserve your going out
and your coming in
From this time forth, and even forevermore.

PSALM 121:1–8 NKJV

Listen to me...you whom I have upheld since you were conceived, and have carried since your birth. Even to your old age and gray hairs I am he, I am he who will sustain you. I have made you and I will carry you; I will sustain you and I will rescue you.

ISAIAH 46:3–4 NIV

They travel lightly whom God's grace carries.

THOMAS À KEMPIS

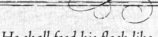

He shall feed his flock like a shepherd:
he shall gather the lambs with his arm,
and carry them in his bosom, and shall
gently lead those that are with young.

ISAIAH 40:11 KJV

His Goodness and Love

The LORD is my shepherd; I shall not want.
He makes me to lie down in green pastures;
He leads me beside the still waters.
He restores my soul;
He leads me in the paths of righteousness
For His name's sake.
Yea, though I walk through the valley
of the shadow of death,
I will fear no evil; for You are with me;
Your rod and Your staff, they comfort me.
You prepare a table before me in the presence
of my enemies;
You anoint my head with oil; my cup runs over.
Surely goodness and mercy shall follow me
All the days of my life;
And I will dwell in the house of the LORD forever.

PSALM 23:1–6 NKJV

Love is the response of the heart to the
overwhelming goodness of God.... You may
be so awestruck and full of love at His presence
that words do not come.

RICHARD J. FOSTER

The goodness of God is infinitely more wonderful
than we will ever be able to comprehend.

A. W. TOZER

*Open your mouth and taste, open your
eyes and see—how good GOD is. Blessed
are you who run to him. Worship GOD
if you want the best; worship opens
doors to all his goodness.*

PSALM 34:8–9 MSG

God's Thoughts

The counsel of the LORD stands forever,
the plans of His heart to all generations.

PSALM 33:11 NKJV

Lord, take my lips, and speak through them;
take my mind, and think through it; take my heart,
and set it on fire.

WILLIAM H. H. AITKEN

For my thoughts are not your thoughts,
neither are your ways my ways, saith the LORD.
For as the heavens are higher than the earth,
so are my ways higher than your ways,
and my thoughts than your thoughts.

ISAIAH 55:8–9 KJV

O the depth of the riches both of the wisdom
and knowledge of God! how unsearchable are his
judgments, and his ways past finding out! For who
hath known the mind of the Lord? or who hath
been his counsellor?

ROMANS 11:33–34 KJV

*Your thoughts—how rare, how beautiful! God,
I'll never comprehend them! I couldn't even
begin to count them—any more than I could
count the sand of the sea. Oh, let me rise in
the morning and live always with you!*

PSALM 139:17–18 MSG

Good Gifts

Rejoice in the LORD your God! For the
rain he sends demonstrates his faithfulness.
Once more the autumn rains will come,
as well as the rains of spring.

JOEL 2:23 NLT

As we grow in our capacities to see and
enjoy the joys that God has placed in our
lives, life becomes a glorious experience
of discovering His endless wonders.

I asked God for all things that I might
enjoy life. He gave me life that I might
enjoy all things.

God has a wonderful plan for each person He has chosen. He knew even before He created this world what beauty He would bring forth from our lives.

LOUISE B. WYLY

Lift up your eyes. Your heavenly Father waits to bless you—in inconceivable ways to make your life what you never dreamed it could be.

ANNE ORTLUND

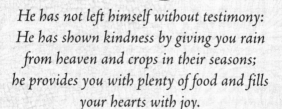

He has not left himself without testimony: He has shown kindness by giving you rain from heaven and crops in their seasons; he provides you with plenty of food and fills your hearts with joy.

ACTS 14:17–18 NIV

Invaluable Love

If you believe in God, it is not too difficult
to believe that He is concerned about the
universe and all the events on this earth. But
the really staggering message of the Bible is
that this same God cares deeply about you
and your identity and the events of your life....
We have missed the full impact of the Gospel
if we have not discovered what it is to be
ourselves, loved by God, irreplaceable in His
sight, unique among our fellowmen.

BRUCE LARSON

For GOD is sheer beauty, all-generous in love,
loyal always and ever.

PSALM 100:5 MSG

Our greatness rests solely on the fact that God in His incomprehensible goodness has bestowed His love upon us. God does not love us because we are so valuable; we are valuable because God loves us.

HELMUT THIELICKE

Let your faith in Christ, the omnipresent One, be in the quiet confidence that He will every day and every moment keep you as the apple of His eye.

ANDREW MURRAY

My God is changeless in his love for me.

PSALM 59:10 TLB

God Speaks

All the absurd little meetings, decisions, and
skirmishes that go to make up our days. It all adds
up to very little, and yet it all adds up to very much.
Our days are full of nonsense, and yet not, because
it is precisely into the nonsense of our days that
God speaks to us words of great significance.

FREDERICK BUECHNER

God talks to those who humbly bring themselves
before Him—young or old—to hear Him speak....
What do you lose by listening to the God who loves
and lives today, who created man and moon and
who wants to walk to you?

BECKY TIRABASSI

For you have exalted above all things
your name and your word.

PSALM 138:2 NIV

Take a moment to consider the awesome
reality that the God who spoke and created the
universe is now speaking to you. If Jesus could
speak and raise the dead, calm a storm...and
heal the incurable, then what effect might
a word from Him have upon your life?

HENRY T. BLACKABY

Be still, and in the quiet moments, listen
to the voice of your heavenly Father. His words
can renew your spirit...no one knows you and
your needs like He does.

JANET L. WEAVER SMITH

*You're my place of quiet retreat; I wait for
your Word to renew me.... Therefore I
lovingly embrace everything you say.*

PSALM 119:114, 119 MSG

Shepherd of Love

God never abandons anyone on whom He has set
His love; nor does Christ, the good shepherd,
ever lose track of His sheep.... We need to "wait
upon the Lord" in meditations on His majesty,
till we find our strength renewed through the
writing of these things upon our hearts.

J. I. PACKER

Abandon yourself to His care and guidance,
as a sheep in the care of a shepherd,
and trust Him utterly.

HANNAH WHITALL SMITH

When at night you cannot sleep,
talk to the Shepherd and stop counting sheep.

Give all your worries and cares to God,
for he cares about you.

I PETER 5:7 NLT

God is the shepherd in search of His lamb.
His legs are scratched, His feet are sore and His
eyes are burning. He scales the cliffs and traverses
the fields. He explores the caves. He cups His
hands to His mouth and calls into the canyon.
And the name He calls is yours.

MAX LUCADO

God is the sunshine that warms us, the rain
that melts the frost and waters the young plants.
The presence of God is a climate of strong
and bracing love, always there.

JOAN ARNOLD

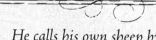

He calls his own sheep by name
and leads them out.... His sheep follow
him because they know his voice.

JOHN 10:3–4 NIV

Love Like That

Watch what God does, and then you do it,
like children who learn proper behavior from
their parents. Mostly what God does is love you.
Keep company with him and learn a life of love.
Observe how Christ loved us. His love was not
cautious but extravagant. He didn't love in order
to get something from us but to give everything
of himself to us. Love like that.

EPHESIANS 5:1–2 MSG

Love has its source in God,
for love is the very essence of His being.

KAY ARTHUR

*I pray that your love will overflow more and
more, and that you will keep on growing in
knowledge and understanding.*

PHILIPPIANS 1:9 NLT